MAYWOOD PUBLIC LIBRARY
MAYWOOD, N. J. 07607

Horses

Published in the United States by
Gloucester Press, in 1979
All rights reserved

Originated by David Cook and
Associates and produced by
The Archon Press Ltd
70, Old Compton Street
London W1V 5PA

First published in
Great Britain 1979 by
Hamish Hamilton Children's Books Ltd
Garden House, 57-59 Long Acre
London WC2E 9JL

Printed in Great Britain by
W S Cowell Ltd
Butter Market, Ipswich

Certain illustrations originally published in
The Closer Look Series

Library of Congress
Catalog Card Number: 78-73839
ISBN: 0-531-03427-5
ISBN (Lib. Bdg.): 0-531-03405-4

Horses

Consultant editor
Henry Pluckrose

Illustrated by
Peter Barrett, Maurice Wilson

Gloucester Press · New York · 1979
Copyright © The Archon Press Ltd 1979

The horse stands to feed.
His teeth grind the grass into pulp.

The horse family includes zebras,
wild asses and donkeys as well as
horses and ponies.
All the animals in the horse family eat grass.
They are called grazers.

The Asian wild ass lives in
the bare plains of Central Asia.

This is a Mountain zebra
from South West Africa.

Once all horses were wild.
They lived in big herds on the grassy plains of Asia.
The horses here are the last of these wild horses.

They are called Przewalski's horse.
They are very rare and most of them
live in zoos.

In North America tame horses which escaped went wild again.
These horses were called mustangs.
The Indians of the American prairies used to catch them and tame them again for riding.

Zebras are really another kind of wild horse.
Their striped skins make them look
very different from other members
of the horse family.
They live in large herds on the African
grasslands.

There are many different types of zebra.
You might think that their black and white
stripes would make the zebras easy to see.
But in the bright African sunlight
the dazzling pattern helps to hide them
from their enemies.

Zebras live in herds, like all wild horses.
The herds move across the grasslands
in search of pasture.
Zebras are food for lions.
They are too big to hide from the lions
so they have to be able to run very fast
to escape from them.

Not all the zebras escape. The young zebras and zebras which are old, sick or injured often become the lion's prey.

Wild asses live in the deserts of Africa, Arabia and Asia.
They live in herds too.
Now they are very rare.
Wild asses are very hardy, sure-footed creatures, for they live in areas where the land is rough and rocky.

The soil is poor and few plants grow.
Water is scarce and sometimes the asses
have to go without water for many days.

The wild asses of Africa are the ancestors of our tame donkeys.
Donkeys are still used all over the world to work for man.

In many countries donkeys pull carts, carry loads and are used for riding. They make good pets too but sometimes they can be stubborn!

Horses were first tamed by people
who lived in the grasslands of Asia.
Descendants of these people still live there
with their herds of horses.
They use horses for riding and for carrying
and for pulling loads.
They milk the mares (female horses).
The horses provide them with meat and skins.

Horses like these were used for centuries by merchants to carry their goods from one town to the next.

Today tame horses live all over the world.
Not so long ago they pulled carts
and coaches and ploughs.
Now horses are mainly used for riding.
There are many different breeds of horse.
The Arab is the oldest breed and the swiftest.
Most racehorses have some Arab blood
in them.

A beautiful Arab horse and a brown, part-Arab racehorse.

Once a year, wild ponies are rounded up and some of them are chosen to be tamed. This pony is being broken in, or tamed. He has to learn to wear a bridle and reins and to carry someone on his back.

Ponies live in a half-wild state on rough land and mountains and are very tough.

Today ponies are used mostly for riding
but once they did all sorts of jobs.
Before cars were invented, ponies
were the only animals strong enough
and sure-footed enough to carry loads
over hills where there were no proper roads.

The pony is popular because it is small and can be safely handled by quite young children. Ponies are also used for pulling small carts and as work horses.

The wild lands where horses and ponies live
are getting smaller as man takes more
of them for his own use.
So the herds of wild horses
are likely to get smaller too.
But tame ponies, horses and donkeys
have a bright future as friends of man.

Horses running free
in open country

Index

Africa, 7, 12, 16, 18
America, 10
American Indians, 10
Arabia, 16
Arabs, 22, 23
Asia, 7, 8, 16, 21

donkeys, 7, 18-19, 28

grazers, 7

herds, 8, 12, 14, 16, 21
horse family, 7

lions, 14, 15

mustangs, 10

ponies, 7, 24-5, 26-7, 28
Przewalski's horse, 9

racehorses, 22, 23
riding, 10, 19, 21, 22, 26

taming horses and ponies, 10, 21, 24, 28

wild asses, 7, 16-17, 18
wild horses, 8-9, 10, 21, 28
working horses and ponies, 20, 21, 22, 26, 27

zebras, 7, 12-13, 14-15